Books should be returned on or before the
last date stamped below.

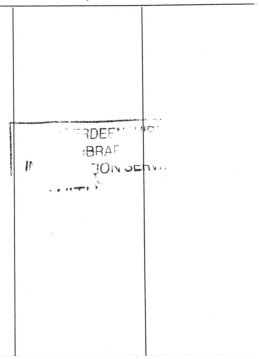

D1426545

Clothes and Fashion
Then and Now

Written by Alastair Smith

Designed by Ruth Russell

Illustrated by Maria Wheatley

Series editor: Judy Tatchell

Long, long ago

Long, long ago, people wore clothes made from animal skins.

They killed wild animals and ate them. Then they used the animal skins to make clothes.

Ooo, I like that!

Thanks. I caught it myself.

Which animals?

Here are some of the animals that people made their clothes out of.

Deer

Bison

Wolf

For cold weather clothes, they used bears' thick furry coats.

Making clothes

People took the skin and stretched it out to dry in the sun.

Pegs keep the skin stretched. →

They used sharp stones to cut the clothes into the right shapes.

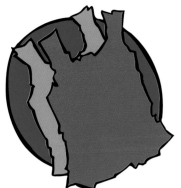

They sewed the clothes with strips of animal skin.

← Animal bone needle

Too hot!

In really warm weather, animal skins were too heavy and hot. People took off their clothes.

When it's hot we wear a lot less!

I wear these clothes all the time. They're really smelly!

Lift the flap to see how things have changed.

3

Whew- it's hot!

In Egypt it can be really, really hot. People wear light, airy clothes that help to keep them cool.

In ancient Egypt, about 4,000 years ago, people mostly made clothes from a cloth called linen. Linen comes from a plant called flax.

Linen thread is woven into cloth on a loom.

Loom

Linen thread

Other fashions

Ancient Egyptians wore jewels, beads and bangles. Here are some of them.

Rings

Bracelets

Necklace

Many men and women kept their hair short. On special occasions they wore wigs.

Most people wore black make-up around their eyes. The make-up was called kohl.

In ancient Rome

Here you can see what people wore in the ancient city of Rome, 2,000 years ago.

Most people wore tunics made from cheap cloth. This boy is wearing a tunic.

Today, people in Rome dress more like this. Nobody wears the old style of tunic any more.

Fine clothes

In ancient Rome, rich people bought silk or cotton clothes. Silk and cotton were rare and expensive.

Today, silk and cotton are not rare, but the best silk is still very expensive.

Shoes

In ancient Rome, shoes were made of leather or canvas. Shoes are still made from these things.

Ancient

Modern

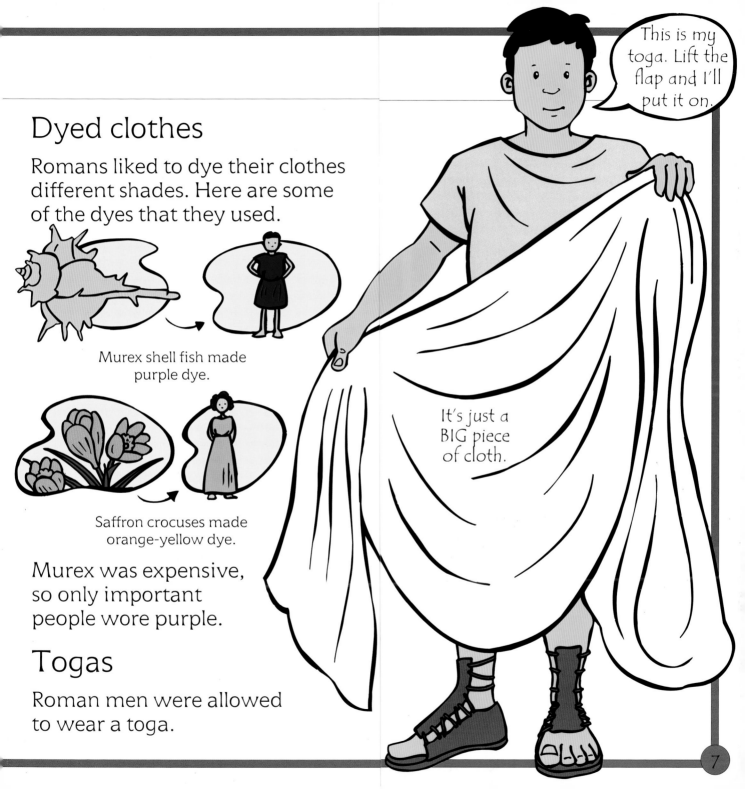

Dyed clothes

Romans liked to dye their clothes different shades. Here are some of the dyes that they used.

Murex shell fish made purple dye.

Saffron crocuses made orange-yellow dye.

Murex was expensive, so only important people wore purple.

Togas

Roman men were allowed to wear a toga.

Brrr - it's cold!

The Vikings lived in a place that can be very, very cold. They had to make clothes that kept them warm.

Here's a Viking woman. To make sure that she stayed warm, she wore lots of layers.

Thick wool shawl

Long tunic, made from wool

Long dress, made from heavy linen

Leather shoes

Clothes from wool

Vikings made a lot of their warmest clothes out of sheeps' wool.

They made the wool into thread by spinning it.

Often, they dyed the thread to make it look nicer.

They made the thread into cloth on a loom.

Loom

We still make lots of clothes out of wool.

Looking good

Vikings made and wore fine beads, bangles and necklaces.

A woman's gold brooch

A necklace made of golden balls

Viking men liked to keep their beards and long hair neat and tidy.

I've braided my beard!

Here's a Viking comb. It's made of a deer's antler.

Viking men

Viking men sailed the seas and explored foreign lands. When it was cold, this is what they wore.

Fur hat

This fur cloak keeps out the icy wind.

Long wool shirt

Thick wool trousers

Viking clothes were warm but heavy.

Dressing up

About 200 years ago, rich people took ages to put on their best clothes. Just look at what they wore.

Beauty patches

Many people wore patches on their faces. They made the patches out of silk or velvet. They glued them on with sticky paste.

The patches covered scars and pimples.

Big wigs

Rich women wore huge wigs. The wigs were made from a mixture of human and animal hair. Some women wore great big hats on top of their wigs.

Make-up

People put white make-up all over their faces, with pink spots on their cheeks.

Do you think he looks nice?

Going out

These people are ready to go out to a party.

The scarf around his neck is called a cravat.

Short trousers show off the lower part of the leg.

Some men wear padding here to make their legs look chunkier.

Clothes for children

About 170 years ago, people wore clothes that looked like these.

Children's clothes often looked like grown-ups' clothes. Girls' dresses weren't as long, though.

Wearing hats

Most children wore hats when they went outside. Would you like to wear a hat like this?

A shorter skirt means that she can run around easily.

This type of hat is called a bonnet.

These days, most children only wear hats when they really need to.

Rain hat to keep the rain off.

Sun hat to keep the sun off.

Wool hat to keep the cold out.

Suits for boys

About 150 years ago, many boys wore suits.

These are my best clothes.

Some wore waistcoats and ties, even when they were playing.

Lift the flap to see what very young boys wore.

This little boy is still in his night clothes.

Time to get dressed.

Most people wore nightshirts like this when they went to bed.

Finishing touches

Look at these things. They've all been very fashionable at some time over the last 3,000 years. You might be able to spot some of them on other pages in this book.

Fantastic hats

German soldier's hat,
450 years old

Giant hat,
200 years old

Brooches, bangles and buttons

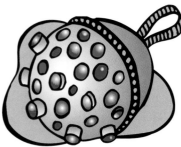

Button with jewel,
100 years old

Viking necklace,
1,000 years old

Silver button,
350 years old

Gold brooch,
200 years old

Clothes for your feet

Woman's high heels,
35 years old

Boy's boots,
450 years old

Man's boots,
250 years old

Man's shoes,
250 years old

Man's hunting hat,
250 years old

Woman's hat,
75 years old

Gold bangle,
3,000 years old

Diamond brooch,
200 years old

Roman man's sandals,
2,000 years old

Girl's boots,
100 years old

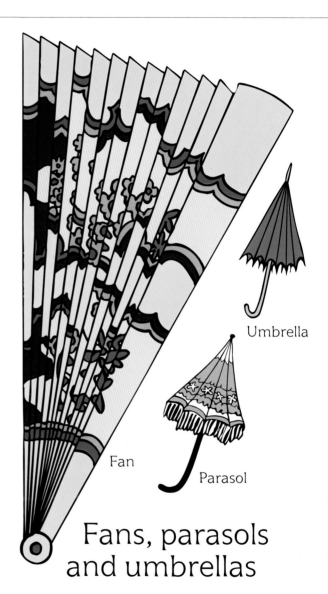

Fan

Umbrella

Parasol

Fans, parasols and umbrellas

All these things are closed, to make them easy to carry. Lift the flap to see them open.

15

Index

With thanks to Dr. Anne Millard for providing the information for this book.

First published in 1999 by Usborne Publishing Ltd, 83-85 Saffron Hill, London EC1N 8RT, England. www.usborne.com

First published in America in1999.   UE

Printed in Hong Kong, China.